GEORGE WASH

A Life from Beginning to End

Copyright © 2016 by Hourly History.

All rights reserved.

Table of Contents

Introduction
The Washingtons of Virginia
Europe Exports its Wars to the Colonies
Washington at Mount Vernon
An Englishman no Longer
Washington at War
The Father of His Country
Return to Mount Vernon
Conclusion

Introduction

In 1783, George Washington's work on behalf of his country seemed to be concluded. He had led his young nation to military victory against overwhelming odds, beating what many had assumed to be the invincible British Army. He had, through force of personality, kept his own forces united when military defeat, lack of supplies, physical hardship and lack of payment could easily have led soldiers to abandon what seemed to be an abstract and futile struggle for freedom. With the war won, it was time for General Washington to return to his native Virginia and leave the American stage that he had dominated for almost a decade. Once the treaty establishing peace between the British and the Americans was signed, he would be his own man again: George Washington, private citizen; husband of Martha Dandridge Custis Washington, the wealthy widow he had married after his return from the French and Indian War; master of Mount Vernon.

But the need for his leadership had not yet passed. While still in charge of the army, he discovered that his military officers planned to mutiny because they feared that Congress would not give them the back pay and pensions owed to them. If that happened, these officers planned to abandon their fellow Americans to whatever might happen if the British decided not to honor the peace treaty. The officers decided that they would march on Congress to obtain what was owed to them, with violence if necessary.

Washington, who had more than once paid his soldiers from his own private funds, had had his own struggles with Congress and its inability to supply its army. But he was not going to let his years of service dissolve into the hostility of a rebellion against an untried government. He ordered his officers to meet him on March 15. The meeting place, the Temple of Virtue, was a large hall near Newburgh. Without fanfare, he slipped into the meeting place and read his nine-page speech. In what would become known as the Newburgh Address, he shared their concerns over their just demands for payment, but he criticized the way in which they intended to achieve their pay. The army had suffered through the war years; he knew, he reminded them, because he had suffered with them and now was fighting their battle with Congress to press for payment. Could they, he challenged, sully the glory they had earned in battle by turning from disciplined soldiers into a mob to march on Congress? He told them to support the building of a government as he intended to do. Civil discontent, he told them, was not the solution. Legislative process to address their grievances was the answer.

But when he began to read from a letter of support written by a Virginia representative who supported the officers, Washington's eyesight proved faulty. As he put on a pair of spectacles, he said, "Gentlemen, you must pardon me. I have grown gray in your service and now find myself growing blind."

His officers, remembering how much Washington had gone through as their leader, were contrite; many were moved to tears. The following day they passed a resolution to commend their Commander-in-Chief for his devotion to his soldiers.

Washington continued to write letters to urge Congress to honor its debt to the Army by paying them the money they had been promised. Through patience and perseverance, his efforts were successful and his officers were given five years of full pay for their service.

This episode, one of many in the life of a man whose code of honor held him to a standard which lesser men would have abandoned, is a telling one. Patience and perseverance, submission to duty, self-discipline rather than self-glory - these were the trademarks of the man whose leadership earned him the gratitude of a nation and the respect of the international audience. When King George III of Great Britain learned that, after his military achievements, George Washington planned to return home rather than seize power in the nation which was so clearly in his debt, the monarch said, "If he does that, he will be the greatest man in the world."

George Washington would have shunned such extravagant praise. But history has affirmed the legacy of a man who, by seeking neither fame nor power, achieved both and in the process, earned the title of Father of His Country.

Chapter One

The Washingtons of Virginia

"I had rather be on my farm than emperor of the world."

—George Washington

George Washington's life is steeped in legend. However, most of those legends are a fabrication by a no doubt well-meaning man, Parson Weems, who apparently thought that the father of his country needed a little more color. Washington didn't chop down a cherry tree; he didn't throw a half dollar across the Delaware River. What he did do, however, is more than enough to gild the saga of a man who defined the character of a nation. But his origins were ordinary, with no indication that from his lineage would arise a man who would lead a rebellion against a mighty empire, command a ragtag army against highly trained troops, or govern a country with a bold political experiment that seemingly had no chance to succeed.

The Washingtons

There was nothing in his geography to indicate that the scion of the Washingtons would be anything but an Englishman. The Washingtons who settled in Virginia had their roots, as most of the Founding Fathers did, in Great Britain. In 1657, George Washington's great-grandfather came to America and settled in Westmoreland County. Virginia, which began with the colony at Jamestown, the first permanent English settlement in North America, would go on to become the jewel of the thirteen colonies, but until the settlers turned to tobacco, the economy would not thrive. In 1619, slaves were introduced to the colonial social structure and with that decision, a way of life was established. War with the native tribes east of the Allegheny Mountains remained a threat, and to settle in Virginia was not to opt for a life of safety and security.

Life in England had been prosperous, and the Washingtons had been given land under the Tudor monarchy of Henry VIII. But when civil war struck and Englishmen were choosing sides between the Stuart kings or Oliver Cromwell and the Puritans, the Washingtons came out on the losing end.

Augustine Washington

The Washingtons did not distinguish themselves in the earlier generations, but that would change with George Washington's father. In 1694, Augustine Washington was born. He would, by virtue of good fortune and hard work, prosper with the growth of tobacco, as he built mills and acquired land and the slaves to work it.

His first wife, with whom he had three sons, died in 1729. By 1731, Augustine Washington was a husband again, this time to Mary Ball, who brought land as her dowry into the match. Their six children, the eldest of which was George, born February 22, 1732, would survive into adulthood. Neither aristocrats nor paupers, the Washingtons, who lived on Pope's Creek, were part of the middle class, but it was a prosperous one; Augustine and the sons from his first marriage had received their education not in Virginia, but at the Appleby School in England.

In 1735, the Washingtons moved to Little Hunting Creek Plantation on the Potomac River. The plantation would later be renamed Mount Vernon. In 1738, when George was six years old, the family moved to Ferry Farm not far from Fredericksburg, in Stafford County, on the Rappahannock River, which allowed Augustine to live closer to one of his businesses, the Accokeek Iron Furnace, where he was one of the managing partners. The family used their other plantations for farming, but Ferry Farm was home. The family actually called this the Home Farm, but it acquired the name of Ferry Farm in later years because it was here that people traveling to Fredericksburg took the ferry to cross the Rappahannock River. The ferry was a convenient means of travel for the Washingtons as well, although they didn't own the ferry.

Crossing the Rappahannock was something Washington did on a regular basis. His early education was received in Fredericksburg from the Rev. James Marye, the rector of St. George's Parish. George would have been sent, as his half-brothers and father had in their youth, to England for his formal education, but in 1743, when George was 11 years old, Augustine Washington died. George inherited Ferry Farm and ten slaves but as a child, he could not claim them until he turned 21. In the meantime, Mary Ball Washington would manage the property. His mother would actually continue to live at Ferry Farm until 1772 when she moved to Fredericksburg, where her daughter Betty lived.

Not for Washington was the luxury of William and Mary for his education; he would have instead to make a living. One of the most useful bequests which he received from his father's estate was set of surveyor's instruments. George's older half-brother Lawrence was his father's heir and he undertook the responsibility of overseeing his younger brother's upbringing. He taught him trigonometry and surveying, but also instructed him in the gentler arts of Virginia society. Lawrence had married well; his wife, Anne Fairfax, belonged to a family of affluence and influence in Virginia. The youth took his social education very seriously. *The Rules of Civility*, a primer for young gentlemen on how they should conduct themselves, provided a foundation for George as he learned how to take his place among the gentry. As a young man, he took fencing lessons and paid for dancing lessons; in his manhood, he was regarded as an excellent dancer. His horsemanship was greatly admired and the long hours he would spend in the saddle as an adult owed much to the skills he learned in youth.

As a ranking officer in Virginia's militia, Lawrence's connection to Admiral Edward Vernon, for whom Mount Vernon was named, steered the young boy toward a military career.

Washington Finds a Career

At the age of 16, George joined a surveying company which was exploring Virginia's western borders. Family ties would prove convenient and only a year later, he was appointed as Culpeper County's official surveyor. The training that he received during the two years he spent surveying Frederick, Culpeper and August Counties not only taught him his trade, but also inspired the mythology which he shared with so many Americans. The frontier lay ahead, land was limitless, and to his mind, colonization of the territory to the west was the nation's destiny.

Although he would feel the lack of education throughout his life, Washington was not unschooled. He had studied with a schoolmaster until he was 15, learning geography, the classics, and mathematics, an important subject for a surveyor. He also learned about tobacco farming and caring for livestock, which were integral to the Virginia agricultural economy. He had, at one point, considered a career at sea rather than on the land, and wanted to join the British Navy, but his family did not support this ambition. Surveying looked to be his career; as a younger son, he had a living to earn.

Lawrence Washington suffered from poor health. When he journeyed to Barbados in the hope that the warmer climate would be of benefit, his brother George was with him. However, George contracted smallpox and had to return home. The disease would leave him with some scarring, but his recovery from the deadly pestilence was another example of how the young man managed to triumph over adversity. In 1752, Lawrence died of tuberculosis; two months later, Lawrence's daughter and heir died, leaving George to inherit Mount Vernon.

Chapter Two

Europe Exports its Wars to the Colonies

"Our army love their General very much, but they have one thing against him which is the little care he takes of himself in any action. His personal bravery and the desire he has of animating his troops by example, make him fearless of danger. This occasions much uneasiness."

—Officer in the Virginia militia

Twenty years old and a landowner, George Washington's future as a Virginian was secure. However, the conflict which had Great Britain and France forever at odds was no longer something that took place across the ocean. Both European powers were jealously protective of their colonies in North America, and the French sought to increase their control by occupying the Ohio Valley, where borders were frequently disputed by the British. The colonists may have thought of the land along the frontier as theirs, but for France and Britain, control of the Ohio Valley and the Ohio River, which joined the Mississippi, was an extension of empire; they would not cede the territory without a fight. The rivers of North America were a better transit system than the rudimentary roads of the colonies, and the plentiful waterways were vital for the transportation of the goods which came from the verdant area.

Virginia Governor Robert Dinwiddie wanted the French to leave the land which was claimed by Britain. In 1753, he appointed George Washington to a new post, adjutant of the Northern Neck of Virginia. His brother had formerly held the position of adjutant general for the colony, but Lawrence's failing health had not permitted him to continue to hold the office. George didn't receive a commission for this assignment, but it introduced him to a military career, something which would have far-reaching effects on his later life and on his country as well.

Washington was 21, ambitious, and eager to prove himself. He was sent to Fort LeBoeuf in Pennsylvania. Governor Dinwiddie had a personal and vested interest in the contested Ohio Valley; Virginia's power elite, including George William Fairfax and George Mason, as well as Washington's half-brothers, were shareholders in the Ohio Company, which had been established in 1749 to promote the settlement of the enormous acreage. But the Ohio Company, with its 200,000 acres between the Monongahela and Kanawha Rivers, was made uneasy by the French encroachment into the land. And, as British subjects, they naturally wanted to evict the French from Great Britain's territory.

Traveling with him from Williamsburg were guide Christopher Gist and a friend of the family, Jacob Van Braam, who was able to speak French. They arrived in the midst of a snowstorm in December and Washington delivered his message to Captain Jacques Legardeur de Saint-Pierre, whose polite reply simply asserted in writing that the French had an incontestable right to the Ohio Valley.

Later that year, in March, Governor Dinwiddie again sent Washington on a mission. The Virginia militia was to return to the Ohio Valley, acting defensively, but with instructors to capture or kill anyone who resisted British rule. Washington's camp was located at Great Meadows. Not very far, in a ravine were the French, who were just as determined to order the English to leave the Ohio Valley. Washington and a party of militiamen and Seneca warriors marched through the night, reaching the French camp at dawn on May 28. Caught by surprise, the French were overwhelmed; 13 were killed, 21 captured. Among the dead was French commander Ensign Joseph Coulon de Juonville.

Informed of the attack, the French commander at Fort Duquesne sent Captain Louis Colon de Villiers, who was the brother of Jumonville, to attack Washington at Fort Duquesne. Accompanied by 600 soldiers and Canadian militiamen and 100 natives, DeVilliers headed for Great Meadow. Washington received reinforcements and fortified his position but with only 400 men, he was significantly outnumbered by the approaching French. Fort Necessity, built as its name implies because a fort was urgently and speedily needed, was in the middle of the meadow, an easy target for enemy fire from the encircling woods.

The siege lasted a single day. The French captured Washington and his forces surrendered. What happened next would loom as a professional failure. Not familiar with the French language, Washington signed the surrender but didn't realize that what he'd signed included a confession that Jumonville had been assassinated.

He was allowed to return home, unharmed, as long as he promised not to build any more forts along the Ohio River, and signed the surrender terms. This was not an insignificant event in a colonial backwater; it became an international incident which helped to ignite the start of the Seven Years' War, also known as the French and Indian War, with British and French forces playing out their traditional rivalry in the New World. The prize for the country that won would be the lands which both England and France wanted to control, those resource-rich, seemingly boundless stretches of fertile soil, deep forests, and the promise of wealth. For the colonists, who of course sided with the British because they saw themselves as British, winning was of paramount importance; they were fighting for their homes. No one guessed, of course, that when the battle against the French ended in 1763, another battle would later follow and the colonists would again be fighting for their homeland, this time against the British.

Washington Builds a Reputation

Washington had found his calling. While during the course of battle he had stood in an exposed area which was the target of French fire, hearing the bullets whistle past - a sound he described as charming - he was unharmed. Washington's surrender to the French would be his last; never again would he surrender a force in battle. English author Horace Walpole wrote, "The volley fired by a young Virginian in the backwoods of America set the world on fire."

Upon his return to Williamsburg in January of 1754, Washington committed his account of his journey to the Ohio Valley to paper, receiving praise from the House of Burgesses for his accomplishments. The governor was pleased with the report, pleased enough to have it published in Williamsburg and also in London, the capital of the British Empire. The publicity that it generated clued the British in to the potential danger of the French presence in the Ohio Valley. It also introduced the young soldier to the British audience.

In 1755, with the honorary rank of colonel, he served with the British Army under General Edward Braddock, who planned an attack on the French at Forts Duquesne and Niagara and at Crown Point. The British professional forces numbered 2,100 men; the colonial militia included 500. Braddock, ambushed by the French and their Native American allies, would suffer mortal wounds from the attack. Washington, however, demonstrated the phenomenal luck which followed him throughout his career, unharmed even though two horses were shot from under him and he sustained four bullet holes to his cloak. The story told by the Washington family is that General Braddock presented the red commander's sash to his aide-de-camp. The symbol of command, bestowed upon a colonial soldier, was significant; the sash would become part of American military legend when it was presented to another soldier who would become a president, Zachary Taylor. The sash would be restored to Mount Vernon in 1918.

Washington was named "The Hero of Monongahela" by Governor Dinwiddie for his courage under fire. He was promoted to the rank of colonel and given command of 1,400 militia with an assignment to patrol the 400 miles of border along the frontier. But Washington found out that command carried its own burdens, as he now had to deal with undisciplined troops and the failure of the colonial legislature to give him the support he needed.

The following year, he was sent on another mission to capture Fort Duquesne, this one under the command of Brigadier General John Forbes. Forbes, with 2000 British regulars and 5000 militia troops, followed Washington's recommendation to travel along the southern border of Pennsylvania

This time, after five years of trying, the British won, and control of the strategic Ohio Valley was claimed by Great Britain. Washington retired from his Virginia regiment in 1758, but he was still interested in a military career. But his journey to Boston to meet with Governor William Shirley, who was acting as commander following the death of General Braddock, did not earn him the commission he sought, although Shirley did agree that lower-ranking British officers should not outrank senior militia officers.

But Washington was unaware that a greater destiny awaited him. He returned home to Mount Vernon, disillusioned with his experience, though eventually it would prove to be a useful one. The British had rejected the man who, in just over 20 years, would accept the surrender of General Cornwallis at Yorktown. Washington also learned much about maintaining a fighting force. He read military manuals and learned to write clear orders for soldiers to follow. He had endured and survived the rigorous life on the frontier, and had learned firsthand how troops needed to be supplied, how a campaign needed to be organized, and how military justice should be delivered. He had overseen the construction of a fort. He had commanded subordinates. He had learned how important training and discipline were for troops. He had learned that in order for an army to succeed, the government needed to provide financial and moral support. He would not forget those lessons. The French and Indian War was George Washington's military university, and he graduated with honors.

Chapter Three

Washington at Mount Vernon

"For in my estimation more permanent and genuine happiness is to be found in the sequestered walks of connubial life, than in the giddy rounds of promiscuous pleasure, or the more tumultuous and imposing scenes of successful ambition."

—George Washington

Having returned home to Mount Vernon in 1758 after resigning his military commission, Washington turned his attention to local matters. He had been defeated in his bid in 1755 to become a member of the House of Burgesses, but in 1758, he was victorious and would serve in the legislature for 15 years.

Sally Fairfax

Washington, occupied though he was with legislative and previously with military matters, was not unaware of the fairer sex. His sister-in-law was a member of the Fairfax family. George William Fairfax, brother of Anne Fairfax Washington, had caught the attention of a young girl named Sarah Cary, whose father was very particular about his daughter's marital options. He approved her marriage to Fairfax, whose father owned more land than anyone else in Virginia. To Cary, this boded well for his daughter's future.

During his life, Lawrence Washington had frequently visited Belvoir, the estate where Sally Fairfax and her husband lived, and George Washington was often with him for these visits. They met when Washington was 16, and by the time of the French and Indian War, he was in love. Even when he was later engaged to Martha Custis, the woman who would become his wife, Washington wrote to Sally that, "The world has no business to know the object of my love, declared in this manner to . . . you . . . when I want to conceal it."

But Sally was married to a man who aspired to the nobility which, years later in 1773, would mean moving to England at a time when colonial Americans were dissolving their loyalty to the Crown. The English Fairfaxes did not endow her husband with a title, nor did they view Sally as a fit match for a Fairfax. Virginia would confiscate the Fairfax family holdings because their stance as Loyalists meant that they were regarded as traitors. In 1798, after the war had ended, George Washington would write to her to encourage her to return to Virginia. Nothing, he wrote, could "eradicate . . . the recollection of those happy moments, the happiest in my life, which I have enjoyed in your company." But Sally stayed in Bath, dying in 1811. Of her feelings for the man whose unrequited love never died, Sally gave no indication, although she once wrote, in a letter to a relative, that "I know now that the worthy man is to be preferred to the high-born."

Love was romantic in colonial America, but it was also practical, as was necessary in a land where people were needed to tame a wilderness. There were other women in Virginia, eligible brides who would be happy to marry the very available George Washington who had distinguished himself in his military service and who was a landowner. One of those eligible brides was the widow Martha Dandridge Custis.

Martha Dandridge Custis

Born in 1731 in New Kent County and the eldest of eight children, Martha Dandridge stood out from many of the Virginian women of the era because she could read and write. In addition to reading the Bible, she also enjoyed novels and magazines, and was, in common with others of the time period, a dedicated writer of letters to family and friends.

A diminutive five feet tall, Martha was regarded as beautiful, accomplished, and well able to conduct herself socially, traits which were prized in colonial Virginia. When she was not yet 18, she met Daniel Patrick Custis at church. Custis, who was 38 years old, lived at the White House plantation located four miles down the Pamunkey River from the Dandridge home. Custis' father opposed the romance just as he had opposed his son's earlier female interests; he was unimpressed with the Dandridge's lower social status and lack of wealth. He threatened to disinherit his son. But Martha won him over, or perhaps he realized that his son was well past the usual age when Virginia men were long since wed. At any rate, the marriage took place.

Upon the death of his father, Custis became even wealthier. Martha, now firmly ensconced as a member of the Virginia upper class, was able to furnish her house in a costly style which included tea sets, sterling silver flatware which bore the Custis coat of arms, damask fabric for the dining room chairs, and fashionable Chinese porcelain. Her wardrobe was stylish, and she even possessed, as a present from her husband, a riding chair, which was a costly one-person carriage lined with blue cloth.

The marriage, said to be a happy one, lasted seven years until Custis died in 1757. During those years, Martha would give birth to four children, all of whom would bear the middle name of Parke. This was in obedience to the condition set by Martha's father-in-law, who decreed that only grandchildren whose names included Parke would inherit part of the estate. Daniel Parke Custis was born in 1751; Frances Parke Custis in 1753; John Parke "Jacky" Custis, born in 1754; and Martha Parke "Patsy" Custis, born in 1756. Martha would outlive all four children: Daniel died of malaria in 1754, Frances in 1757. Jacky and Patsy, who suffered from seizures, would die at the age of 27 and 17, in 1781 and 1773, at a time when Washington had little time for domestic matters, even those which affected his family.

For a woman of wealth, widowhood had its appeal. Custis had died without a will, which left his widow as the executor of his estate, giving her a freedom few women had and even providing her with some of the same legal rights possessed by men, including the right to buy and sell property, make contracts and bring a legal suit to court.

Even in mourning, Martha had to meet her obligations. She contacted merchants in England to direct them that, because of her husband's death, future correspondence should be sent to her. She oversaw the harvesting and shipping of the tobacco crop. She addressed outstanding legal matters with consultation of attorneys. She even lent money to planters in the neighborhood and set up the repayment schedule. She also had a three-year old son and a year-old daughter to care for. It was understood that she would eventually remarry. Martha had another advantage denied to most colonial women; because of her wealth, there was no reason to marry for financial security. Martha was free to fall in love.

Washington Finds a Wife

After her husband's death, Martha was 26 years old, the owner of 17,500 acres of land and almost 300 slaves, a financial inheritance worth more than £40,000. In the Virginia marriage market, the Custis widow was a prize.

George Washington was also a marital prize, with his military reputation and his land, particularly Mount Vernon. Virginia society was closely knit and the news of the attractive young widow likely spread fast. George called on her in March, 1758. Less than two weeks later, he visited her again, making the 35-mile journey to her home before returning to his military post. It wasn't long before they were planning their marriage; Washington worked to renovate Mount Vernon while Martha ordered a trousseau from London.

The couple married in January 1759. Martha's trust in her new husband was evident from the beginning when she did not seek to protect the assets of her Custis marriage from him with a premarital contract, as was her option. During her lifetime, Washington would have the use of her "widow's third," which consisted of the land, slaves, and money which would be inherited by the Custis heirs after their mother's death. He was also the legal guardian of Jacky and Patsy Custis, managing their financial affairs and protecting their Custis assets.

In Virginia a plantation like Mount Vernon, which consisted of eight thousand acres divided into five individual farms, was both home and business for its owners. Many of its 300 slaves were artisans skilled as bricklayers and carpenters, farm laborers, ditch diggers, drivers for the wagons and carts, gardeners, cooks, and dairy maids; the seamstresses, butlers, domestic staff and footmen who made up the household staff were likewise slaves.

Washington was not born to an idle life and he was firmly invested in farming. He farmed for profit, but in doing so he was an avid student of agriculture. Virginia's main crop was tobacco, but when he realized that it was hard on the soil and wasn't sustainable, he turned to wheat as a cash crop in 1766. He practiced the new techniques that he had learned about including crop ration and different methods of fertilization.

As a member of the Virginia gentry, the Washingtons enjoyed an active social life which included fox hunting, the theatre, playing cards and billiards, dancing, and fishing. He also continued to attend to his civic duties, becoming a justice of the peace in Fairfax County in 1760. The Washingtons moved in the highest circles of Virginia society and entertained liberally, particularly during Christmas when they celebrated the holiday with friends who gathered to enjoy their generous hospitality. Martha's meat pie, which included turkey, chicken, goose, partridge, pigeon, woodcocks, and hare, was a holiday favorite, as was the "great cake", a fruitcake liberally soaked in brandy, with ingredients that included 40 eggs and four pounds of butter.

Chapter Four

An Englishman no Longer

"The British Government hath no more right to put their hands into my pocket without my consent, than I have to put my hands into yours, for money."

—George Washington

George Washington was born an Englishman in colonial Virginia and there was no expectation or interest in loyalty to any other nation. A British heritage was something of which to be proud. But there were stirrings of discontent among the colonists. British rule saw that the purpose of the colonies was to supply the other country with raw materials and, in turn, import English goods. But there was an ocean between the mother country and her vigorous, growing offspring, and the colonies found their own ways around England's rules. That growing independence in matters of trade would eventually seep into other areas of colonial thought as well.

The British in Control

The turning of a blind eye to colonial enterprise which dominated half of the 18th century changed after the British emerged the victors in the French and Indian War.

A rebellion by an alliance of the Ottawa, Huron and other native tribes in 1763 and the British counterattack led to a treaty which promised that colonial migration beyond the Appalachian Mountains into Indian Territory would be forbidden. But the Proclamation of 1763, by setting a defined western boundary with British posts established to regulate the border, required colonial settlers who had moved beyond the boundary to abandon their settlements. To make matters worse, the colonies themselves would be required to pay for the British posts monitoring the frontier. To the colonists, not only were they being denied the freedom to venture west, but they were charged with the payment for the force which denied them the freedom to move.

The French and Indian War had been expensive. It had drained the British coffers, and it seemed reasonable that the colonies should bear the expense of replenishing the treasury by paying taxes levied by Parliament. The colonists disagreed, and the response "no taxation without representation," expressing their disagreement at being taxed but having no voice in Parliament, would serve as the foundation of their simmering discontent.

British Legislation and Colonial Discontent

Already incensed that the British Parliament had intervened in their geography by establishing western boundaries to the frontier, the colonists were outraged when the Stamp Act passed in 1765. The act initiated a tax with the aim of raising money to support a standing army of British soldiers who would be stationed in the colonies, and was the first internal tax levied against the colonies for financial transactions taking place within their own boundaries. Items taxed included newspapers and advertisements in newspapers, court documents, playing cards, dice and other items. The Stamp Act Congress met in 1765 to express their disapproval of the legislation; their disapproval took the form of a decision to boycott British goods. Some irate citizens were more proactive in expressing their reaction to the tax, and the homes of tax collectors, as well as the custom houses themselves, were sometimes attacked.

Outrage against the Stamp Act was not confined to New England. In Virginia, the House of Burgesses, under the leadership of Patrick Henry, passed the Stamp Act Resolutions which affirmed the rights of the colonists, as English subjects, to give their consent to taxation before it was implemented. Henry was inclined to go a little further in his vehemence than other members of the legislative body and the resolution stated that any attempt to assume the power to impose taxes would tend to destroy both British and American freedom. Clearly, the Boston firebrands would have their counterparts in the Old Dominion.

In 1765, representatives from nine of the 13 colonies met in New York. Known as the Stamp Act Congress, this group, the first united body of the colonial representatives, endorsed the Virginia resolutions. The body was not defiant; the representatives sent expressions of affection to the King and the government, but nonetheless asserted that, as British subjects they had the right to have representation if they were going to be taxed. The following year, reacting to the protest, Parliament repealed the Stamp Act.

But in 1767, Parliament passed the Townsend Acts, which taxed glass, lead, paper, and paints and tea that the colonies imported from Great Britain. Again, the colonists viewed the taxes as tyranny and a violation of their rights as English subjects. Their response was to limit the items that they imported from Great Britain. This was not the response that the British government wanted; American markets for British goods were part of their economy. The government repealed the duties imposed by the Townsend Acts except for the one on tea; the tax was a small one, and the British felt the need to establish their authority to tax their colonies as they chose.

British soldiers were sent to Boston when the Townsend Acts roused rebellion. The colonists refused to accept imported British goods which were taxed by the government. In 1770, the discord between Boston citizens and British soldiers resulted in the death of five colonists who would come, in what was described as the Boston Massacre, to be regarded as the first casualties of the imminent American Revolution. Except for a few far-thinking and volatile Patriots, the colonies were not yet envisioning themselves as independent of Great Britain.

But Parliament had not repealed its view that it had the right to tax its citizens, whether or not they were represented in the London government. Great Britain had its own economic purposes for taxation; in 1773, the East India Company was in financial trouble and needed help. Parliament passed the Tea Act, which was designed to lower the tax on tea and give the East India Company a monopoly of the tea trade in the colonies. This would make it possible for the East India Company, with its cheaper tax, to undercut the tea that the Dutch smuggled into the colonies. In Charleston, South Carolina, the tea was unloaded and stored in city warehouses for three years. New York and Philadelphia turned the tea ships back and forced them to return to Great Britain. But in Boston, the mood was more incendiary. The Patriots were determined that the tea, valued at £15,000, would not be unloaded. Boston acted swiftly. One December night, dressing up as Mohawk Indians, colonists dumped the tea into Boston Harbor.

In March 1774, Great Britain responded with what the colonists would call the Intolerable Acts. Parliament closed the port of Boston and placed Massachusetts under military rule. Virginia and Maryland showed solidarity by boycotting British exports and imports. There was some self interest in the measure because the Chesapeake region had been in the midst of a recession since late in 1772 due to a decline in tobacco prices. Withholding tobacco from sale allowed them to wait out the price decline until their crop was more profitable.

Another of the Intolerable Acts alarmed the other colonies. Parliament required the Massachusetts colonial government to obtain the approval of the governor before towns could hold meetings; appointments for councils would be by appointment rather than election. The other colonies were suspicious of this development, seeing in the response by the British a forecast of what could easily transpire in the other colonies if they incurred the displeasure of Parliament.

The Colonies in Rebellion

In September, 1774, twelve of the thirteen colonies were represented by 55 men who gathered in Philadelphia at the First Continental Congress. They elected a Virginian, Peyton Randolph, as president. Patrick Henry, also a Virginian, objected to the decisions to vote by colony when they make resolutions; he stated that the representatives should vote as Americans. The purpose of this First Continental Congress was not to govern in place of Great Britain, but to perform as ambassadors to issue protests and adopt resolutions.

By the time the Second Continental Congress met in May of 1775, American militiamen had met British soldiers in combat at Lexington and Concord, Massachusetts. Blood had been spilled; the British were in control of Boston. Events turned the provisional gathering into a revolutionary government.

A month after the gathering began, realizing that the colonies were now at war with Great Britain, the representatives were obliged to assess this new development. John Adams nominated George Washington as general and commander-in-chief of the Continental Army, and the Congress approved unanimously. Washington was the obvious choice because of his experience in combat during the French and Indian War. He was a man of honor, respected by the leaders of the government; a man who inspired respect. Washington accepted the assignment, with the condition that he was not to receive a salary for his position. But he had doubts that he would be able to accomplish the task.

Chapter Five

Washington at War

"I had no hesitation to declare that I had but one gentleman in my mind for that important command and that was a gentleman from Virginia, who was among us and very well known to all of us, a gentleman whose skill and experience as an officer, whose independent fortune, great talents, and excellent universal character would command the approbation of all America and unite the cordial exertions of all the colonies better than any other person in the Union."

—John Adams

Before leaving to take command of the Continental Army, Washington wrote to Martha to explain his decision. "You may believe me, my dear Patsy, when I assure you . . . I have used every endeavour in my power to avoid it, not only from my unwillingness to part with you and the family, but from a consciousness of this being a trust too great for my capacity, and that I should enjoy more happiness in one month with you at home than I have the most distant prospect of finding abroad."

Washington Takes Command

Washington took command at the direction of the Second Continental Congress, but in truth there was no army. The individual colonies, now states, had militias which were not coordinated under any single central authority. There was no national fighting force because there had been no nation. The means for transporting troops, supplying them and feeding them, did not exist. There was not even a military tradition for these nonprofessional soldiers to understand or conform to authority from on high. The Continental Army would be matched against the trained, experienced, and paid government-supported soldiers who had proven themselves in conflicts across the Empire.

The effects of the hostilities appeared instantly. There were rumors of slave uprisings, always the fear of the slave-holding population. The British enlisted slaves in their army and Virginia's royal governor offered freedom to slaves who left their masters and agreed to bear arms against them. The economy began to show the effects of the boycott against British goods, compounded by the blockade which Parliament had ordered. Hard currency became difficult to obtain in the colonies because goods weren't being sold.

These were matters for the new government to address. Washington had more than enough to do as the commander of the fighting force. Washington's experience in the Virginia militia and his service with the British Army during the French and Indian War had taught him the military techniques of soldiering. His first task was to organize. From the jumble of militias, Washington organized an army of three divisions, six brigades, and thirty-eight regiments. Eventually, Congress would provide some support by ordering the states to supply regiments which were proportionate to their populations.

The first battle of the war, Bunker's Hill, was fought on the day that Washington was named commander. Fought by Massachusetts militiamen, the victory went to the British but with 1,000 casualties, it was not an auspicious opening for Great Britain. In January 1776, the American forces began to bombard the British in Boston. The Continental Army, planning an advance to Dorchester which overlooked Boston, began to build fortifications. The British were stunned by the rapid colonial advance. British plans to attack Dorchester had to be cancelled due to the winter weather, but they tired of waiting. Rather than attack, the 9,000 British troops and 1,100 Loyalists decided to leave Boston, first dumping their weapons into the harbor.

Subsequent encounters would not be so easily resolved. By August, the new country had formally declared its independence and had a national flag. What they didn't have was a formula for victory.

British General Henry Clinton defeated the Continental Army at Brooklyn, New York with a flanking motion which was nearly successful in capturing Washington. However, Washington was able to evacuate 9,000 troops along with equipment and horses across the

East River, surprising the British who were unaware that their quarry had escaped.

But in November, the Continental Army, now encamped at Morristown, New Jersey, was reduced in numbers. Then Congress offered $20 and 100 acres of land for any man who signed up for a three-year enlistment or the duration of the war. Those incentives attracted much-needed recruits to fill the ranks.

There were critics of Washington's command and even calls for his removal. Washington wasn't just fighting the British, he was also fighting his political enemies - including fellow Virginian and General Charles Lee, who believed that others would be more successful in command of the Continental forces.

Washington and His Winter Soldiers

But, as always, Washington maintained his composure. During a trying winter, Washington had words from Thomas Paine read aloud to the soldiers. Paine had published *The American Crisis* in 1776, writing that while the summer soldiers and the sunshine patriots would fail their country, those who withstood the times that tried men's souls would earn the love and gratitude of their countrymen. Paine's words didn't provide the suffering soldiers with food or respite from the cold, but the soldiers were reminded that their battle was for something intangible that would enrich their nation for generations to come if they stood fast to their mission.

Washington and some of his officers, recognizing the need of their soldiers, paid them out of their own private funds. The soldiers suffered greatly. There were times when there was not enough food for the men and their horses. Some of the men lacked shoes and clothing. But even in the midst of such privation, the training continued. Baron von Steuben had offered his services to the Continental Army and he instituted vigorous training and discipline routines. He drilled the troops and his efforts inspired morale along with confidence.

On December 25, 1776, overnight, Washington and his force of 2,400 men crossed the Delaware in the midst of a snowstorm. They reached Trenton, New Jersey at dawn, surprising the Hessian garrison that had spent the night in holiday revelry. Only 500 Hessians were left alive and uncaptured; Washington's wounded numbered six.

Washington was not in command at the Battle of Saratoga, New York, the following year, but British General John Burgoyne surrendered to American General Horatio Gates and later returned home to London to a frosty reception. 5,700 British soldiers were imprisoned in Virginia. When the French learned of the victory, the American quest for an alliance and military support was met with a more favorable audience.

Help would be needed. Another winter awaited, even worse than the previous one. Disease broke out, food was in short supply, and desertions abounded. Washington warned an unresponsive Congress that if it failed to provision the military soon, there would not be an army left to fight. In order to supply his starving forces, Washington sent two generals to confiscate livestock from local farms in Delaware, New Jersey and Maryland, offering in exchange receipts which promised reimbursement by the Continental Congress.

The news that the French were amenable to an alliance bolstered support and morale for the fight. France recognized American independence and granted trade concessions to its new ally, along with special shipping privileges.

One of Washington's skills was in making the best of his resources, limited though they were. He was able to hold his army together. He supervised his generals well. He maintained cordial relations with Congress and worked well with the states, their governors and their militias. He was always mindful of the logistics of the war. And he insisted on training.

Washington's generals included men of skill but also men of ego. Artemus Ward, Charles Lee, Philip Schuyler and Israel Putnam were his major generals. Seth Pomeroy, Richard Montgomery, David Wooster, William Heath, John Sullivan and Nathaniel Greene were commissioned brigadier generals. Horatio Gates, who was appointed adjutant general, was given the rank of brigadier. The defection of General Benedict Arnold to the British was a strategic blow to the American cause but also a blow to morale. The fact that the plot, which involved Arnold turning over the West Point garrison to the British, was discovered when the British spy Major John André was captured, minimized the potential of Arnold's treason, but it shocked the soldiers and the nation.

victory. Cornwallis decided to take his troops to Yorktown.

By October, Cornwallis' army was besieged by the forces of Washington and French troops under the command of the Comte de Rochambeau. French naval forces on the York River trapped the British in the middle. On October 19, 1781, Cornwallis surrendered.

Chapter Six

The Father of His Country

"About 10 o'clock I bade adieu to Mount Vernon, to private life, and to domestic felicity, and with a mind oppressed with more anxious and painful sensations than I have words to express, set out for New York . . . with the best dispositions to render service to my country in obedience to its call but with less hope of answering its expectations."

—George Washington

Although the British Army had surrendered, the Continental Congress needed to have a military force ready to act in case of hostilities until the formal peace treaty ending the war was signed. George Washington remained in command until the Treaty of Paris was signed in 1783. He accepted the transfer of power from the British troops in New York. After bidding farewell to his own troops in New York, a scene which saw battle-hardened soldiers and the normally impassive Washington both in tears, General Washington went before the Continental Congress to resign his commission. Stopping at Philadelphia, he submitted the list of expenses, totalling $63,315 that he had paid out of his own money to support the war and his troops.

It took him four days to travel the three hundred miles to reach Mount Vernon in time for Christmas. While in Philadelphia, he had purchased Christmas presents for his family, which not only included Martha but also the children of Jacky Custis, who had died of camp fever after the Battle of Yorktown, leaving Eleanor and George Washington Parke Custis to be adopted by Jacky's mother and stepfather.

Washington was a stickler for duty, and when his country required him, he served. But he was also devoted to his estate and the agricultural obligations that were upon him as a landowner. He had been able to return to Mount Vernon only once during the years of war and at that time he had seen how neglect had made inroads against his careful maintenance.

At the age of 51, he perhaps assumed that he would retire to his plantation to concentrate his remaining years upon his estate and his family. It was no doubt a joyous homecoming, but his return to his beloved Mount Vernon was destined to be a short one, despite Washington's intent to live out his days as a private citizen.

Washington's passion for order was not exhibited solely in his goals to restore Mount Vernon. He also wished to see the country he had helped to create establish a strong government. The Articles of Confederation under which the nation operated failed to create a government which operated as a single entity.

Washington is Called to Serve as President

The Constitutional Convention in Philadelphia was called to solve these problems but also to establish a precedent for governance which would honor the American principles of liberty while validating its means of guaranteeing freedom.

Washington, who had struggled to keep an army in the field while a weak government was unable to support it, knew better than anyone what risks lurked in the future for a powerless central government. He knew that a standing army was a necessary player in a nation's ability to defend itself and secure its borders. He also knew that without a strong executive at the helm, the nation would quickly fall prey to powerful international enemies.

The new nation had much to resolve: how to balance the wishes of the more populous, powerful states with the needs of the smaller ones; how to establish a central government which did not override the independence of the separate states; how to create a nation which would not be ruled by kings, but would govern as a republic. And perhaps most importantly, who would lead this new experiment in government? Americans recognized that only one person could serve as the first president of the United States. He was the man who had not sought power, but had responded to the call of duty, the man who had relinquished military command when an army was no longer needed, and had returned home when his mission had ended.

On February 4, 1789, in a unanimous vote, the 69 members of the Electoral College chose George Washington to serve. Creating a new government was on his shoulders and Washington was aware that this was a monumental task. The journey from Mount Vernon, Virginia to New York City, the nation's capital where he would be inaugurated, took seven days. The oath of office was administered on April 30 by Robert Livingstone, New York's highest ranking judge, because the Supreme Court did not yet have justices to assume that role.

Washington Builds a Government

Washington knew that in order to govern effectively, he needed the advice of able ministers. There was no formal process, such as now exists in American government, for designating Cabinet secretaries and in the beginning he would seek reports from the men he had selected to serve in leadership roles. By the end of 1791, he was convening meetings with increasing frequency with the heads of the executive departments. He himself did not participate in the discussion, instead leaving the debate to the ministers. Those ministers were: Thomas Jefferson, Secretary of State; Henry Knox, Secretary of War; Alexander Hamilton, Secretary of the Treasury; and Attorney General Edmund Randolph. Washington prized unanimity but his former colleagues and brothers-in-arms were not as united as they had been during the war. The four men, reflecting Washington's painstaking efforts to instil balance in government, represented different regions of the country: Jefferson and Randolph were

Virginians; Knox was from Massachusetts; and Hamilton was a New Yorker.

The interests of North and South almost immediately rose to conflict between Hamilton and Jefferson over the establishment of a national bank. Hamilton was determined to see that the United States was established on a solid financial foundation. Washington supported Hamilton in this aim and agreed that the national debt should be funded and state debts incurred during the war should be assumed by the federal government, but the hostility between Hamilton and Jefferson was bitter and acrimonious.

They represented different hopes for the future of America. Jefferson cherished the agricultural heritage of the country; Hamilton looked to manufacturing and industry to build the nation. Jefferson believed in the judgement of the people and the sovereignty of the states; Hamilton was suspicious of the majority, and believed that only a strong central government could effectively wield power. Hamilton's zeal for a national bank stemmed from his belief that financial security solidified public and international trust.

Their different views would, in the end, lead to the development of political factions which would represent partisan views and create political parties. This was far from Washington's dream for his country, but he had done what he could, and what no other man could have, to create a nation founded both on ideals and pragmatism. It would be up to his successors to maintain what he had built.

There were times, however, when Washington recognized the need to act on his own, without guidance from his Cabinet or input from Congress. He was wary of conflicts in Europe and when France and Great Britain went to war in 1793, he issued the Declaration of Neutrality. When Western Pennsylvania farmers rebelled against the establishment of a federal tax on whiskey, he led a military force to put down the revolt.

Martha Washington was no less a trailblazer in her role as the wife of the president, a position which would later become known as the First Lady, although during her tenure she was usually referred to as Lady Washington. The social responsibilities of the president's wife were not entirely unlike those of a Virginia aristocrat, although the atmosphere was probably more circumscribed. She made social calls and hosted Friday evening receptions attended by dignitaries and members of Congress, behaving, as did her husband, with impeccable propriety and courtesy. Martha, who was an inveterate writer of letters, once confided to a niece that being the wife of the president was akin to being a state prisoner.

Washington's terms in office were spent in New York City and Philadelphia, but the next president would serve in a new capital, to be located on the Potomac River, and named Washington City, in honor of the nation's first president. Looked at superficially, the establishment of the capital named for the nation's first president was a noble gesture of gratitude. But the tenor of the decision was more in line with the partisan wheeling and dealing which would dictate national politics when Washington was gone from office.

Hamilton agreed to a deal with James Madison. If Madison helped get Hamilton the votes he needed in the House of Representatives to pass the Funding Act so that the federal government could assume the states' war debts, Hamilton would lobby for support to locate the nation's capital in southern territory, along the Potomac River. This would assuage the fears of the South that Northern economic might would supersede Southern influence. Washington would not govern in the new nation's capital, but Washington D.C. would be the capital of the United States.

Chapter Seven

Return to Mount Vernon

"I cannot tell you, My dear friend, how much I enjoy home after having been deprived of one so long, for our dwelling in New York and Philadelphia was not home, only a sojourning. The General and I feel like children just released from school or from a hard taskmaster, and we believe that nothing can tempt us to leave the sacred rooftree again, except on private business or pleasure."

—Martha Washington, 1797

The return of the Washingtons to Mount Vernon was a restoration of a domestic life which had been denied to them for a long time. Restoring their estate to order required effort on both their parts, and Washington would spend the remaining years of his life in overseeing the repairs while he worked to make Mount Vernon not just their home but also financially solvent. In addition, they were once again involved with family and friends, entertaining members of Virginian society and enjoying their grandchildren.

But in 1798, politics once again intruded upon their private life at Mount Vernon, when President John Adams appointed Washington as commander-in-chief of the country's military force. The appointment came because of tensions with France, the former ally during the American Revolution, had grown to threaten invasion of the United States. Washington's assignment took him from Mount Vernon for one six-week trip. Delegating some of the responsibility to Alexander Hamilton, his second-in-command, Washington was able to coordinate some of the military preparations while home at Mount Vernon. Fortunately for the nation and for the couple, Washington did not have to go to war; Adams was able to negotiate a peaceful solution that averted conflict.

In 1799, Martha's favourite granddaughter, Nelly Park Custis, married George's nephew, Lawrence Lewis, in a ceremony at Mount Vernon. The newlyweds lived with the Washingtons while their home was being built.

Washington's Death

Washington wrote in his diary on December 12 1799 that snow began at ten o'clock, followed by hail and then a cold rain. Nonetheless, he spent five hours outside on horseback inspecting the grounds of Mount Vernon. A sore throat the following day developed into illness. Doctors were called and as was customary, proceeded to bleed him. Washington apologized for causing trouble, and he died on December 13, around midnight.

He left an estate worth $500,000 to Martha for use during her lifetime, after which it would pass to his nephew, Bushrod Washington. To his slave William, known as Billy Lee, who had served with him throughout the war, Washington bequeathed $30 for every year of his life in return for his faithful service. Washington had purchased Billy Lee, then a teenager, as a valet in 1768, and the slave had been at Washington's side during the war. He had been with Washington in the thick of battle in case the General needed a fresh horse or a telescope with which to view the action. He was renowned as an excellent horseman, a talent which he had honed when he accompanied Washington on fox hunts in peacetime.

Upon Martha's death, all his slaves were to be given their freedom. His grandchildren received farmland in Virginia. To his five nephews, he left his swords and the instructions that they were never to be unsheathed to shed blood unless in self-defense or in defense of their country and its rights. His friends were given gifts from his personal belongings. He left money for a school for the poor and orphaned children, and money to build a national university in Washington D.C.

Slavery was a complicated institution both morally and economically for slave owners. Martha intended to obey the instructions of the will but after Washington's death, following fires of undetermined origin at Mount Vernon, the family decided that it would be better to free the slaves that George Washington had owned at once.

He had requested a simple funeral, but the nation which mourned his passing would see him off in appropriate style, with a band playing, a ship anchored in the Potomac firing a grand salute, and thousands of mourners in attendance at the services. Perhaps there was no one, before or since, who has matched the stature of the nation's first president, but no one could deny that George Washington earned the praise which described him as "First in war, first in peace, first in the hearts of his countrymen."

Conclusion

George Washington had fought his battles - it would be up to another generation altogether to solve the dilemma of slavery. But the legacy of George Washington has endured in the United States from the first moment when he appeared on what would be the national stage as the only man who could possibly lead his country to independence.

What other men of lesser ego did not always understand about Washington was that his own personal code of honor required that, above all, he should do his duty by conforming to his own firmly entrenched ethics. He wanted his name to be recognized as that of a man who served his country. He wanted his country to continue to uphold its heritage where freedom was cherished.

George Washington had no children, no sons or daughters born to him. America was his child, and he raised his offspring as carefully and attentively as he would have done had he been a father. It forever remains for America to express its adherence to his lessons.